WALKING

GRAFHAM WATER

Number Eight in the popular series of walking guides

Contents

Walked, Written and Drawn by Clive Brown

Published by Clive Brown
ISBN 978-1-907669-08-8

PLEASE
Take care of the countryside
Your leisure is someone's livelihood

Close gates
Start no fires
Keep away from livestock and animals
Do not stray from marked paths
Take litter home
Do not damage walls, hedgerows or fences
Cross only at stiles or gates
Protect plants, trees and wildlife
Keep dogs on leads
Respect crops, machinery and rural property
Do not contaminate water

Although not essential we recommend good walking boots; during hot weather take something to drink on the way. All walks can easily be negotiated by an averagely f person. The routes have been recently walked and surveyed, changes can however occur, please follow any signed diversions. Some paths cross fields which are under cultivation. All distances and times are approximate.

The maps give an accurate portrayal of the area, but scale has however been sacrificed in some cases for the sake of clarity and to fit restrictions of page size.

Walking Close To have taken every care in the research and production of this guide but cannot be held responsible for the safety of anyone using them.

During very wet weather, parts of these walks may become impassable through flooding, check before starting out. Stiles and rights of way can get overgrown during the summer; folding secateurs are a useful addition to a walker's rucksack.

Thanks to Angela for help in production of these booklets

Views or comments?
walkingcloseto@yahoo.co.uk

Walking Close to
Grafham Water

Since it was opened in 1966 by the Duke of Edinburgh, Grafham Water has become a popular leisure area. Crowds of people all day and every day take advantage of the excellent facilities to sail, windsurf, fish, cycle, walk or just have a gentle stroll then sit down and enjoy a cup of tea. It was created during the early sixties by damming the shallow valley of Diddington Brook. Most of the water it contains is pumped from the river Ouse at Offord.

The reservoir is home to a wide range of wildlife; some unusual flora and some reclusive animals that live in the woodland close by. It is however the birds that attract most attention; a tremendous variety are coming and going through the seasons in addition to a large resident population, making it close to heaven for birdwatchers. The Cormorant for instance, primarily known as a sea bird is a frequent visitor.

There is a well made, easily walked path/cycleway stretching for 10 miles right around Grafham Water, it is accessible from each of the four car parks but also goes through the less well known parts, past the nature trials and close to the dragonfly pond. It is also very popular with cyclists of course, so be aware of them while using it. The walks in this booklet make some use of this path, but go beyond the immediate boundaries of the reservoir and into the surrounding countryside; from secluded woodland where you can nevertheless still hear the muted roar of the A1 or the A14 to farmland almost devoid of trees and virtually silent.

The walks can be accessed from several other points and the astute walker will realise some of the walks may be joined together to form a longer expedition.

The maps give an accurate portrayal of the area, but scale has however been sacrificed in some cases for the sake of clarity and to fit restrictions in page size.

All rights of way can easily be negotiated by an averagely fit person.

We feel that it would be difficult to get lost with the instructions and maps in this booklet, but recommend carrying an Ordnance Survey map. All walks are on Explorer Map No. 225; Landranger No. 153 covers at a smaller scale. Roads, geographical features and buildings, not on our map but visible from the walk can be easily identified.

1 Madders Hill

5³/₄ Miles   3 Hours

Use the car park at the bottom of Church Road out of Grafham, no toilets, pub in the village (1 mile). The walk will be muddy in wet weather, best in summer when the ground is hard.

1 Go out of the back of the car park, past the barriers bearing left on the hardcore track to a signpost at a single metal bollard and follow the track right. Continue uphill, under the old bridge and down the slope to the marker post on the right.

2 Turn right along the field edge and go through the boundary. Just before the wood, go through the gateway to the left and turn right to maintain the original direction with the hedge then the wood on the right. At the marker post turn right over the footbridge and follow the obvious track to the left through the trees. Continue over the next footbridge and down the left hand side of the field. Keeping the same overall direction carry on between the trees, over the footbridge and down the tree lined track to the road.

3 Turn left along the grass verge of this surprisingly busy road, around the double bends to the driveway signposted to the right; turn right, down to the marker post at the end. Turn diagonally to the right across the field which may be under cultivation, the path should be visible within the crop but if not it is difficult to follow. Walk for 300yds and then turn right to the to the footbridge partially obscured in the hedge ahead. Cross and continue up Madders hill, the path straight on, should be visible through the crop.

4 At the tarmac road along the top of the hill turn left, walk past the ruin of Redwood Lodge and through the gap in the hedge to the left of the pond. Maintain direction through the next hedge gap and across the field to the wood.

5 Turn right and walk on keeping the wood to the left, turn left over the footbridge and then right along the opposite side of the hedge/dyke. Continue over the next footbridge to the road.

6 Keep direction along the bridleway almost opposite to the right, past the caravan site; turn left then right at the marker post and walk down the edge of the field with the wood to the right. Go through the field boundary; turn left at the next boundary back onto the outward path under the disused railway bridge and back to your vehicle.

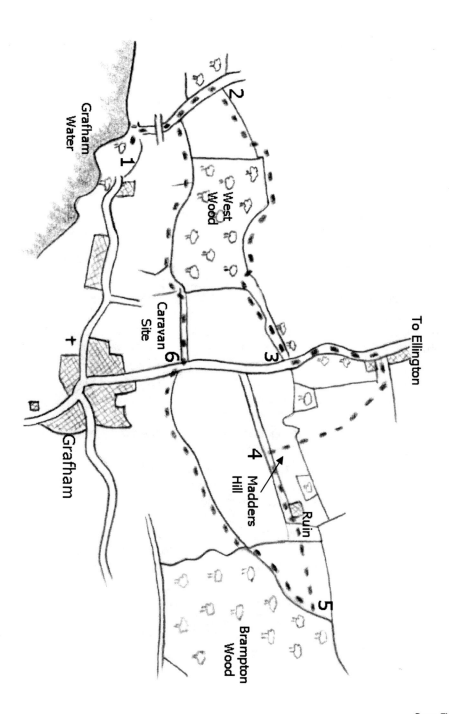

2 Midloe

6½ Miles   3½ Hours

Park in the Plummer car park (pay and display) on the eastern side of
Perry, toilets on site, other facilities at the main (Marlow) car park closer to
Grafham village.

1 Walk to the east along the hardcore path anti-clockwise around the lake, go
past the end of the dam to the road. Turn right for a short way to the footpath sign
on the left. Follow the path between Farm and field with the hedge to the right.
Turn right along the farm road and follow as it turns left, in front of some modern
chalet bungalows.

2   Keep direction along this hardcore road to a marker post and turn right then
left around the field. In the next corner, turn left where the road goes right and
continue past an information board, about Midloe Grange, to the next marker post
and turn right. Carry on across the tarmac farm road and turn right at the corner.

3 Continue with the trees on the right through a gateway, then between open
fields. Follow the track round to the left and to the right at a marker post. Maintain
direction now on this green bridleway, it crosses a farm road, goes around a double
bend and bears right before reaching a road.

4 Turn right and go straight on at the junction, through the scattered buildings of
Dillington and turn right at the signposted footpath.

5 Cross this field diagonally to the far corner on a path roughly halfway between
the two nearer telegraph poles, the path should be visible although the field may be
under cultivation. Go over the footbridge and continue along the field edge, skirting
around the end of a dyke, up the increasing slope. Keep direction through the
trees, past the mast. Turn right then left around the next field, carry on through
the gap between hedge and trees. Cross the stile to the right and turn left down
the side of the field, go over two stiles to the left of the water tower and down the
path to the road and walk across.

6 Turn right past Buckden Court and continue on the path next to the road; just
before the iron railings at the derestricted signs follow the cycle path to the left, and
then right through the trees. This path winds its way through the undergrowth back
to the Plummer car park and your vehicle.

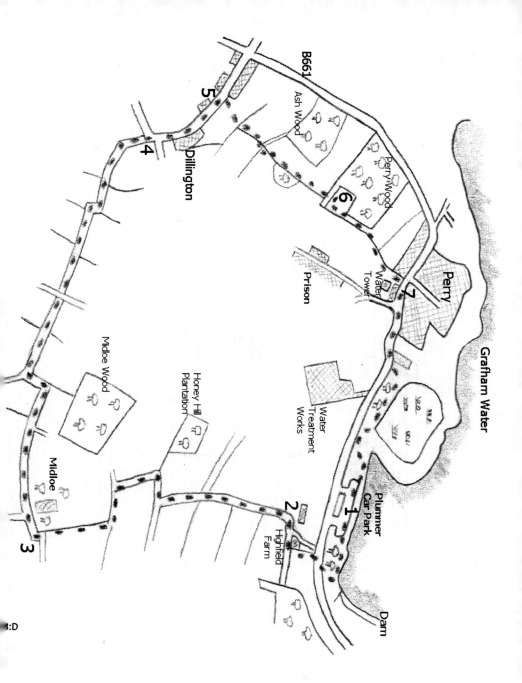

3 Staughton Moor

5¹/₂ Miles   2¹/₂ Hours

Find a parking space in Great Staughton, limited parking at weekends available close to the school on The Causeway. No toilets, local pubs the 'White Hart' and 'The Tavern'

1 Take the Footpath south of the Main Road opposite the sundial and Laura's Close. Cross the stile to the right and go down the path between hedges. Go over the stile to the right then turn left to the original direction and continue with the hedge on the left. Step over the stile in the top corner, turn right and walk down to the river. Turn left along the riverbank and keep going over the next stile. This section can be quite overgrown and the river may not be visible. Turn right over the footbridge then left along the opposite bank and go through the wide hedge gap.

2 Turn right down the edge of the field, hedge and dyke to right. Bear right at the road, follow to the left and go straight on as the road turns sharply right. Walk down the bridleway on a slight left and turn sharp left before the summit of the gentle rise.

3 At the triangular clump of trees turn right uphill along the hardcore bridleway. The farm road goes into a dip next to a reservoir. The path leaves the farm road at the field boundary and crosses the field diagonally right, the path should be visible but the field may be under cultivation. Maintain direction across a farm track to a footbridge.

4 Continue down a wide grass track between two fields and the left hand side of the next field, dyke and trees to left. Go through the farmyard to the road. Keep direction along the road and at the T-junction for another quarter of a mile to the footpath sign on the right.

5 Turn right and follow the track between fields. Cross the footbridge half hidden to the right at the bottom of the dip, turn right for 50yds then left up the slope. Go through the gap in the hedge and turn left along the edge of the field. Turn right in the corner along the field edge with the hedge to the left. Continue down the hill past the trees onto the concrete road and to the right of Garden Farm. Bear left over the cattle grid to the road.

6 Turn right and walk past the church and over the River Kym to the B645 and your vehicle.

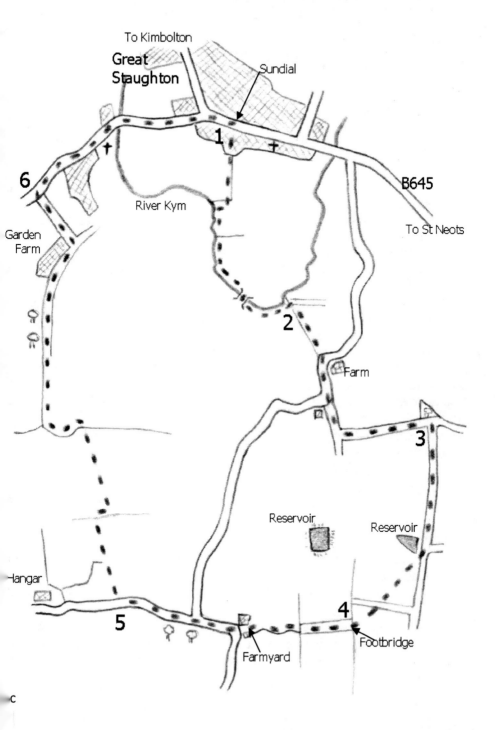

To Kimbolton

Great Staughton

Sundial

River Kym

B645

To St Neots

Garden Farm

6

1

2

Farm

3

Reservoir

Reservoir

Hangar

5

4

Farmyard

Footbridge

c

4 Cockway Lane

$6^1/_2$ Miles   3 Hours

Find a parking space in Spaldwick village. Start from the green triangle in the village centre. No toilets. Pub, The George Inn.

1 Go into the churchyard. Walk past the church door to the stile on the left. Step over the stile and cross the field diagonally left to the kissing gate. Go along Royston Road opposite and continue down the hedged track between the school and the bungalow, cross the stile at the end and head for the next stile hidden in the hedge opposite, more or less in line with the farm buildings. The track should be visible in the grass. Go over the bridleway and the footbridges and keep going to the farmyard.

2 Take a slight right here and get back to the original direction along the edge of the field between the pylon and the hedge. Cross the field ahead at a slight diagonal right in the direction of the marker post to a footbridge the handrails of which may just be seen, the track should be visible through the crop. Continue with the hedge on the right, through the narrow clump of trees, down the right hand side of a field then after 50yds change sides to walk in the same direction with hedge on left. Cross the footbridge and maintain direction over the field ahead which may be under cultivation. Take the bridleway straight on at the crossroads of farm roads.

3 At the marker post turn right, through the wide hedge gap and follow the dyke and then a hardcore bridleway into the village of Stow Longa.

4 Turn right into the village and then left into The Lane just a little further on. Go through the gate at the bottom and down the fenced track; carry on along a more substantial farm road. Take the right at the fork, bear right at some trees and maintain direction through a hedge gap to the road.

5 Walk to the right along the wide grass verge of the B660.

6 After 300yds turn right into Cockway Lane (signposted Three Shires Way). This hardcore road goes past a house and becomes a delightful green bridleway leading all the way back to Spaldwick ($2^1/_2$ miles), the church soon comes into view straight ahead.

7 Approaching Spaldwick, the track becomes tarmac and there are bungalows either side. On the left just before the Mount Pleasant sign is an almost hidden stile, cross and go over the field diagonally right to the stile by the church crossed on the outward route.

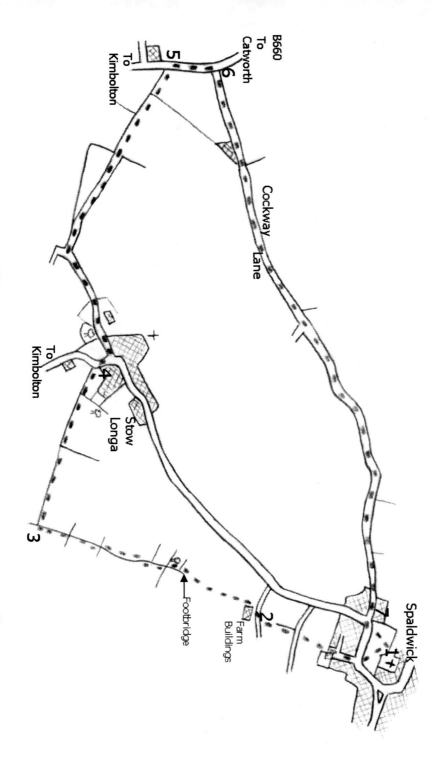

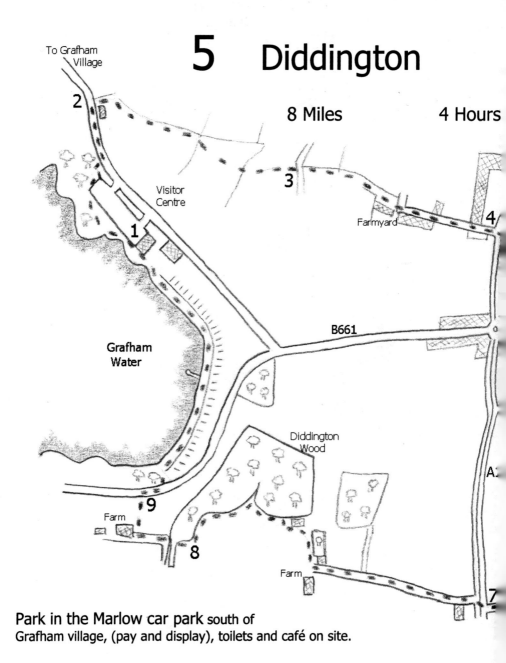

8 Miles   4 Hours

To Grafham Village

2

Visitor Centre

1

3

Farmyard

4

B661

Grafham Water

Diddington Wood

9

Farm

8

Farm

7

A.

Park in the Marlow car park south of
Grafham village, (pay and display), toilets and café on site.

1   Go to the top right hand corner of the car park furthest from the visitor centre, either by the path next to the lake (turn right/anti clockwise) or between hedge and trees. Cross the stile, turn left and walk along the road for 400yds.

2 Turn right at the footpath sign just past the cottages. The path bears right along a farm road and then carries on down the left hand side of the field, hedge and dyke to the left. At the top corner follow the field edge to the right; turn left almost immediately through the gap and right again for 20yds. The path crosses the field to the left at a diagonal close to 45°, more or less in line with the largest of the trees. This field may be under cultivation but the track should be visible within the crop.

3 Cross the field boundary and continue direction down the left hand side of the field to the right with the hedge to the left, carry on over the boundary and the farm road on the left hand side of the next field. This section of the walk may be very overgrown and tough going, go through hedge gap by marker post, continue through the farmyard and the kissing gate to the road. Carry on ahead to the Great North Road.

4 Cross carefully, turn left along the grass verge and then right into High Street. Walk past the Spread Eagle, the George, the Lion and the Vine; the Great North Road comes into view again. Turn left into Mayfield and continue as it becomes Lucks Lane.

Buckden

Pond

6

5 Turn left down the footpath almost opposite The Osiers. Go across the road, past the houses and turn sharp right at the junction of paths away from the pond. Cross the footbridge, turn left at the road and walk past the Cranfield Way sign. Turn right for 25yds and then left at the footpath sign between the bungalows, the path goes to the right along the rear of the gardens, crosses into the field and continues direction along the edge of the field with the hedge to the right.

6 Go over the narrow road and keep going with the hedge still on the right as the path bears gently right. It joins a farm road for a few yards and then turns left with it through a gap in the hedge ahead. Continue on this road into the village of Diddington; follow the road through the village turning right at the corner, to the Great North Road.

7 Cross this busy road carefully and maintain direction along the tarmac road almost opposite. Walk to the end (three quarters of a mile), between the house and the farm and turn right down the tarmac bridleway. Bear left in front of the cottage, follow the fence and then go left along the edge of the field, trees to the right. Keep going around the edge of the wood; ignore the broad gap to the right.

Turn right at the corner of the wood by the marker post and carry straight on through the gap at the next marker. Walk up the farm road and turn right just before the farm, along the edge of the field, with the hedge on the left.

Completed on the next page (Fourteen)

9 Cross the road and the shallow dyke, walk to the right for a few yards, turn left and go through the gate at the end of the dam. Continue the length of the dam past the visitor centre to the car park and your vehicle.

---

6 Fiddler's Acre

$4^1/_2$ Miles $2^1/_2$ Hours

Park in Kimbolton, toilets, shops and pubs on High Street.

1 Start from the High Street. Walk to the east towards St. Neots; the road goes around two sharp corners. Turn left over the concrete bridge crossing the river Kym. 250yds down this track, another track joins from the left, turn right here through a field entrance. Cross the field ahead, the path should be obvious although it may be under cultivation, to a point just to the right of the large clump of trees. Keep direction over the next field to the footbridge to the right of the telegraph pole.

2 Turn left and walk up the hill on the left hand side of the field, hedge on the left, for a few yards over a mile. Go through the tree lined avenue to the left of Fiddler's Acre wood and on to the road.

3 Bear left and then right almost immediately through the gateway. Follow the path signposted across the field to the opposite corner; the path should be well marked if there is a crop in the field. Go around the gate and down the edge of the field, fence to right. Continue past the pumping station gates and along the concrete roadway to the marker post.

4 Turn left at a fairly sharp angle (see map) down the path, which should be well marked to the road. Walk to the left on this road for 50yds and then follow the path signposted to the right on a concrete road. Continue along the road as it curves right; bear left at a T-junction towards Kimbolton church spire, half hidden in a dip in the middle distance. The road rapidly becoming rougher with grass growing through the cracks, bears gently left and then sharp right beyond a gap in the hedge.

5 Keep on the road ignoring the first T-junction and turning left at the next, up to but not on to the road.

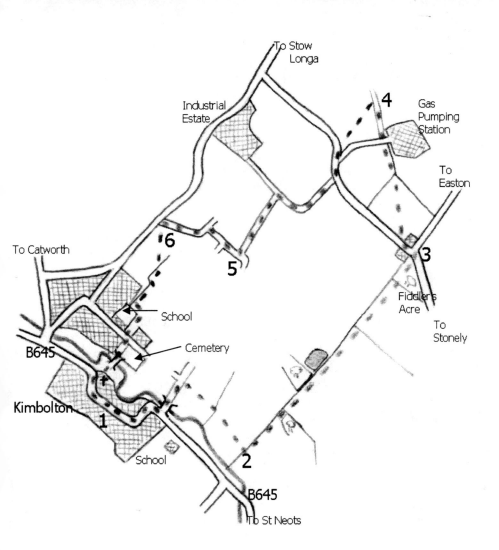

Cross the field to the left in the signposted direction, the track should be visible through any crops. Go through the gap in the hedge, turn right and continue along the field edge, following the hedge to the left then the right around the school. Go to the right of the white cottage and carry on down the wide path between the cemetery wall and the hedge. Turn left at the end, cross the footbridge to the right and continue straight on to the road. Turn to the left into Kimbolton and your vehicle.

D

7   Agden Green

5 Miles   2$\frac{1}{2}$ Hours

Park in Mander car park at the western end of West Perry, off the B661 to the south of Grafham Water, pay and display, toilets, refreshments and shop on site. Pub, the 'Wheatsheaf' on the main road.

1   Leave the car park by the vehicle entrance, go back to the road, turn left and walk into the village. Pass the Wheatsheaf Pub and take the footpath signed to the right immediately after the bus shelter.

2   Cross two stiles within the next 50yds and continue down the right hand edge of this field. Go over the stile to the right but keep to the original direction between the hedge and Perry Wood, walk past the open space, turn right at the trees and then left through the gap at the marker post. Carry on past the wire fence around the phone mast and along the left hand field edge. Approaching the field boundary, cross the dyke to the left, go over the farm road and maintain original direction along the next field edge with the hedge on the right. At the boundary of this field, the path goes diagonally right towards the left hand side of the clump of trees almost hiding the houses to the right.

3   Turn right at the road through the hamlet of Dillington, go straight on over the crossroads for half a mile and turn right at the bridleway signposted Three Shires Way.

4   When the bridleway turns right at the farmhouse carry on through the gap in the hedge and maintain direction between fields alongside a dyke and then a hedge. The path turns to the right at a marker post and follows a wider track to the wood.

5   Take the left hand path at the trees and then go right at the corner of the wood keeping it to the right. Join and continue along the hardcore bridleway as it emerges from the wood and carry straight on as it turns left not far on. Turn very slight right and continue between hedge and wood, follow the path to the right at the corner. Carry on across the clearing and under the electric cables.

6   Turn right along the hardcore path. (An information board here on the left gives an option of a half mile loop through Littless Wood on a Nature Trail). Follow this hardcore/tarmac path around several corners to Mander car park and your vehicle.

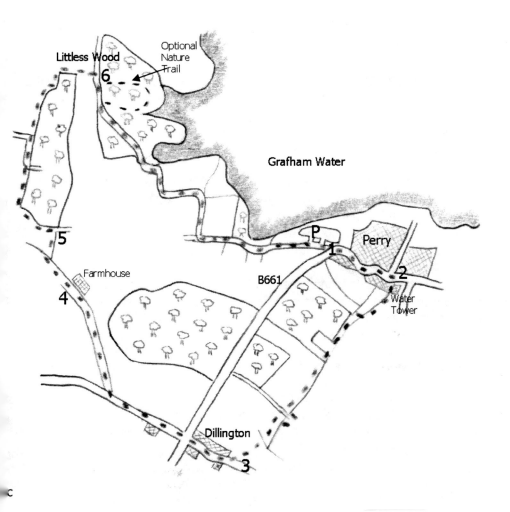

Littless Wood

Optional
Nature
Trail

6

Grafham Water

5

Farmhouse

4

P

1

Perry

2

B661

Water
Tower

Dillington

3

c

8 Hartham Street

$6^{1}/_{4}$ Miles   3 Hours

Park in the car park at the bottom of Church Road out of Grafham, no toilets, pub in the village (1 mile).

1   Leave the car park from the far end; go through the gate and along the hardcore path with the lake to the left. The path eventually turns right through a gate and into the trees, go through the wood and turn right as the trees end. Continue on the path around a narrow stretch of water jutting out of the main lake. On the opposite side of this inlet follow the power lines parallel to the path to an obvious junction just past a pylon.

2   Turn right here up a double track hardcore farm road, passing another smaller pylon. At the top of the slope turn right with the road and keep direction along the joining concrete road.

3   Turn right along Stocking Lane, the Easton to Stonely road; go through a dip and over the hump of an old railway bridge. Turn left at the signpost over the field to the other side of the hedge. The field may be under cultivation but the path should be visible. Bear right along the field edge, past Stocking Barn, through the gate to the right and continue the original direction along the hardcore farm road, the hedge now to the left. As this road turns to the left, carry on across the field in the direction of the church ahead, the track should be visible through any crop. Continue diagonally over the next field to the left of the tree; join and keep general direction along the bridleway to a crossroads of paths.

4   Turn right and walk down the edge of the field hedge to the right; through the boundary and then the hedge lined bridleway to Easton. Turn to the right, at the telegraph pole before the farm buildings, walk down the field edge with the dyke and the hedge to the left. Cross the footbridge in the corner and turn left; continue to the next footbridge, cross and turn right; follow the field edge round to the left and go through the gap to the other side of the hedge. Keep direction with the hedge to the left up to the road.

5   At the road, turn right, ignore the first turn left; take the second left signposted Three Shires Way, which is Hartham Street a hardcore, tree lined public byway. Go left through the gateway after 300yds and continue; finally going up a slope, along the side of a field, down another enclosed track under the disused railway bridge and back to the car park and your vehicle.

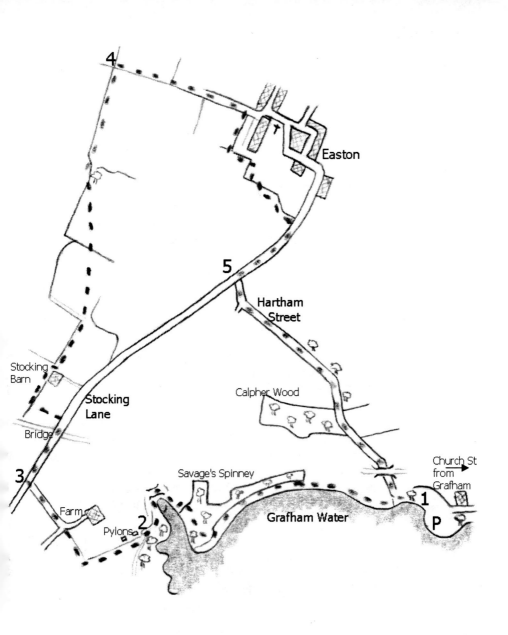

Easton

5

Hartham
Street

Calpher Wood

Stocking
Barn

Stocking
Lane

Bridge

3

Savage's Spinney

Farm

Pylons

2

Grafham Water

Church St
from
Grafham

1

P

9   Gimbers End

7¹/₂ Miles   3³/₄ Hours

Find a parking space in Great Staughton, limited parking at weekends available close to the school on The Causeway. No toilets, local pubs the 'White Hart' and 'The Tavern'.

1   Start from the sundial on the Highway, walk to the west, as the road turns right towards Kimbolton, carry straight on towards Little Staughton. Take the footpath to the right before the bridge, turn left at the marker post level with the houses to the right and follow the edge of the field to the river. Carry on along the riverbank, taking care not to miss a rickety footbridge mostly hidden in the hedge to the left. Keep to this bank do not cross the wider footbridge. Walk to the far corner of the sewage works.

2   Turn left across the concrete road, continue down the hardcore bridleway with the hedge to the left and turn diagonally right along the green bridleway. Follow this track as it turns left, between trees and hedge and then between open fields, back to the river.

3   Turn right and keep to the edge of the river not the wildlife bank between path and crop. Pass one field boundary, at the next just past an unsafe iron footbridge; go straight on between dyke and field. Cross the dyke midway and continue to the corner and turn left down the edge of the field with the hedge to the right. Walk into the tiny settlement of Gimbers End, past the signpost, briefly along the riverbank again, down the side of the field, turn right then left past the houses and onto the tarmac path.

4   Turn right along the path which widens into a road. Walk 50yds to the path signposted left, follow the fence on the right of the field and cross the stile. Go over the corner of the well tended lawn to the left (this is still the path), keeping the hedge on the left go through the fence gap and over the grass to the road.

5   Turn left and then right into the gateway just before the bridge, turn left and walk around to the corner to the right. Go 75yds up the gentle slope to the telegraph pole. Turn right and cross the field at a slight diagonal to the left, the track should be visible although there may be a crop in the field. Carry on up and over the hill, across the footbridge and the next field to the road.

Completion on the next Page (Twenty Two)

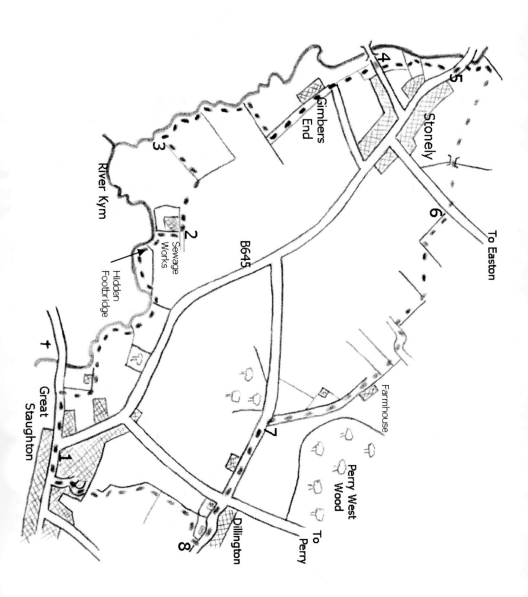

River Kym

Great Staughton

Hidden Footbridge

Sewage Works

Gimbers End

Stonely

To Easton

B645

Farmhouse

Perry West Wood

To Perry

Dillington

1   2   3   4   5   6   7   8

Completion of Walk No 9 Gimbers End from page Twenty

6   Go over the road and the stile almost opposite and continue along the right hand side of the field, turn left at the corner and right through the hedge gap. Cross the field ahead at a slight diagonal, just to the left of the telegraph pole with the yellow notice. The path should be visible within any crop. Go to the low corner of the hedge, through the gap and continue with the hedge on the left through the gap in the next hedge and turn left. Walk into the corner and turn right, along the edge of this field, with the dyke to the left and go through the hedge gap. Maintain direction now along the hardcore bridleway, past the farmhouse and the cottages to the road.

7   Turn left and go straight on at the crossroads, as the houses end turn right at the footpath sign.

8   Follow the path to the right down the backs of the gardens. Turn left at the corner along the edge of the field hedge to the right, at the bottom turn left then right over the sleeper footbridge. Keep to the fenced track as it bears right and continue down the left hand edge of the field. Go left in the corner, right at the next corner and then keep direction to the houses; go through the gap and around the corner into Moory Croft Close, left into Beachampstead Road and up to the B645.

Also by Clive Brown:-

'Easy Walking in South Bedfordshire and the North Chilterns

Published by the Book Castle @ £8-99
37 walks in your favourite style

Notes

The 'Walking Close to' Series

Peterborough
The Nene near Peterborough
The Nene Valley Railway near Wansford
The Nene near Oundle
The Torpel Way (Peterborough to Stamford)
The Great North Road near Stilton

Cambridge
Grafham Water (Huntingdonshire)
The Great Ouse in Huntingdonshire
The Cam and the Granta near Cambridge
Newmarket
The Isle of Ely

Northamptonshire/Warwickshire
The Nene near Thrapston
The Nene near Wellingborough
The River Ise near Kettering
The Nene near Northampton
Pitsford Water
Rockingham Forest
Daventry and North West Northamptonshire
Rugby

Leicestershire
Rutland Water
Eye Brook near Uppingham
The Soar near Leicester
Lutterworth
The Vale of Belvoir (North Leicestershire)
Melton Mowbray
The Welland near Market Harborough

Lincolnshire
The Welland near Stamford
Bourne and the Deepings
South Lincolnshire

Suffolk
Lavenham in Suffolk
Bury St Edmunds
The Stour near Sudbury
The Orwell near Ipswich
Dedham Vale
Stowmarket
Clare, Cavendish and Haverhill
Southwold and the Suffolk Coast

Hampshire
Romsey and the Test Valley

Essex/Hertfordshire
Hertford and the Lee Valley
The Colne near Colchester
Epping Forest (North London)
Chelmsford

Wiltshire/Bath
The Avon near Bath
Bradford-on-Avon
Corsham and Box
The Avon near Chippenham

Bedfordshire/Milton Keynes
The Great Ouse near Bedford
The Great Ouse North of Milton Keynes
Woburn Abbey

Somerset & Devon
Cheddar Gorge
Glastonbury and the City of Wells
The Quantock Hills
The East Devon Coast (Sidmouth, Branscombe and Beer)
Exmouth and East Devon

Norfolk
The Norfolk Broads (Northern Area)
The Norfolk Broads (Southern Area)
The Great Ouse near King's Lynn
North West Norfolk (Hunstanton and Wells)
Thetford Forest
North Norfolk (Cromer and Sheringham)

Nottinghamshire
Sherwood Forest
The Dukeries (Sherwood Forest)
The Trent near Nottingham

Oxfordshire/Berkshire
The Thames near Oxford
The Cotswolds near Witney
The Vale of White Horse
Woodstock and Blenheim Palace
Henley-on-Thames
Banbury
The River Pang (Reading/Newbury)
The Kennet near Newbury

Cumbria
Cartmel and Southern Lakeland

Hereford and Worcester
The Severn near Worcester
South West Herefordshire (Hay-on-Wye and Kington)
The Malvern Hills